CORSTORPHINE

CORSTORPHINE

A Pictorial History of a Midlothian Village

W.G. Dey

F.R.I.B.A.

MAINSTREAM
PUBLISHING

First published in Great Britain in 1990 by
MAINSTREAM PUBLISHING COMPANY (EDINBURGH) LTD
7 Albany Street
Edinburgh EH1 3UG

Reprinted 1992

ISBN 1 85158 366 1

A catalogue record for this book is available from the British Library

Typeset in Goudy
Printed in Great Britain by Butler & Tanner Ltd, Frome

ACKNOWLEDGMENTS

THE BOOK CONTAINS approximately 160 photographs, many of which formed the illustrations for talks which I have given for more than forty years on 'Old Corstorphine'. The material for these talks came largely from contact with men and women who were part of the Victorian and Edwardian era.

Such were John and George Wallace, the clothiers, George Smith, joiner, Davie Duncan, builder, John, Jimmy and Jessie Dey (cousins of my father), who kept a stationer's shop opposite the top of Manse Road and were stalwarts of the Literary Society for over thirty-five years, James Hunter of Manse Road, William Brown of Sycamore Terrace, and many, many more.

My thanks, too, are due to some contemporaries like Mr and Mrs Stoddart, of North Gyle Drive, George Beach, Dr Cormack and Arnie Beveridge, for information hidden from layman's eyes in legal documents, and to Miss Rena Cowper, for her kind remarks in the Foreword and for keeping us all correct regarding historical facts.

Finally, my thanks are due to Mrs Helen Beveridge who has coped with my handwriting and typed the captions for the book and my wife, also a Corstorphine native, who has provided comment and put up with me for over fifty years.

W. G. Dey
Corstorphine, April 1990

FOREWORD

TO THE VIEWER no special pleading is needed to launch this collection of photographs which present a visual, social history of Corstorphine. The collection speaks for itself and its compiler. It is the rich harvest of a lifetime interest in the village and later city suburb where Mr Dey was born and where he has lived his life.

His professional career as a highly respected Edinburgh architect had its correlation in his private interest in photography. Some of the photographs here are his own work, others are those of early exponents of the art whose efforts Mr Dey's seeing eye has preserved for posterity.

The subject-matter is varied, covering the many aspects of life in a rural community. Here are the faces of those who shaped a way of life into which we are now privileged to look. The camera, used sensitively and imaginatively, gives what the printed word cannot give — a visual realisation of human life with all its humour and its pathos.

Happy viewing.

A. S. Cowper BA (Hons) Lond. FLA, FSA Scot.
Corstorphine, April 1990

INTRODUCTION

CORSTORPHINE is now a suburb of the City of Edinburgh that is notorious for its traffic blocks and congestion but at the beginning of this century it was an entirely separate village governed by its own Parish Council. G. Upton Selway called it *A Midlothian Village* when he wrote its history exactly a hundred years ago. This village concept held well into this century and even today there is a community spirit much stronger than in other suburbs surrounding the city. This is probably largely due to the Old Parish Church, dating from the early fifteenth century being at the centre of the district, and which is still in use and to which the other churches owe their origins.

The origins of Corstorphine can only be the subject of conjecture. It is known that in Roman times there existed two roads in the area. One ran north and south carrying traffic from the Roman station at Newstead, near Melrose, across the Pentland Hills at Fairmilehead, making for Cramond by way of a narrow piece of dry land that lay between the Corstorphine and Gogar Lochs, and this would have been crossed by another Roman road running east and west from Musselburgh to Falkirk. This crossing place must have been near the site of our village and it is reasonable to assume that some kind of trade would have arisen from the resulting increase in traffic and that our ancestors would be alert to make something of it. Traces of both roads have been found in recent years. Another reason for an early settlement is that in the area of the old village it is possible to find water readily by sinking a comparatively shallow well; indeed, this was the main source of water for the village until 1880 when a piped supply was brought in from Torduff Reservoir in the Pentlands.

These, then, may have been the reasons for the development of Corstorphine before recorded history but there is a Charter of David I who, after founding the Abbey of Holyrood in 1128, attached to it the church of St Cuthbert's along with that of 'Crostorfyn'. This was a small Norman building called St Mary's which stood on the site of the north aisle of the present Corstorphine Church and served as the Parish Church until 1646 when, according to the Kirk Session Records, it was taken down and some of its stones used to build the porch at the west side of the church tower.

The next reliable date we have is 1376 when another existing deed or charter records the sale of the Barony of Corstorphine to Adam Forstar, or Forrester, a former Provost of Edinburgh. Adam Forrester was a man of wealth who had his town house in Forrester's Wynd in the High Street, where George IV Bridge is now. He also had property in other parts of the town. Adam's thought in acquiring the lands of Corstorphine was to improve the defences of the city by building a defensive castle between the two lochs. It would also be his own house, and during the remaining years of the fourteenth century he did just that. It was a substantial place, having curtain walls 100 feet long with corner towers, each twenty-one feet in diameter and forty feet high. The domestic quarters of the castle were built against the south side of the enclosing walls and served the Forrester family for over

KIRK LOAN
An avenue to the 'low' village.

300 years. During the years that his castle was being built, honours and Crown appointments were showered upon him and he became, in succession, Customar of the Exchequer, Keeper of the Great Seal of Scotland, and a knight, as well as an ambassador to the English and French courts.

Sir Adam died on 13 October 1405 having erected in the previous year a votive chapel in the churchyard near the existing Parish Chapel of St Mary's but quite detached from it. The precise site of this chapel is not known for certain but one suggestion is that it may have been the part which is now the vestry. With a vault below, the living quarters above would have been supported on corbel stones which exist today.

It was Sir Adam's son, Sir John, and his mother, Dame Margaret Forrester, who, after conducting negotiations with the Pope for many years, eventually got permission to found a Collegiate Church of Corstorphine. This entailed enlarging Sir Adam's votive chapel and building what we know today as Corstorphine Church, endowing it to provide not only for the saying of masses for the family, but also for the education of priests to carry on the teaching of the Church.

Sir John and his successors lived in turbulent times and the Forresters' castle had to withstand many a siege in the fourteenth and fifteenth centuries. Indeed, Sir John's son, also Sir John (who was buried in the chancel of the church too), led troops at the siege of Branxton Castle in 1446 and, in revenge, the castle was laid waste by Chancellor Crichton in the following year to the extent that Sir John had to carry out extensive rebuilding works.

Our connection with Mary, Queen of Scots, is somewhat tenuous. It would seem that the castle was one of the few places in which she never slept but it is recorded that she was captured in 1567 by Bothwell's men about two miles west of the village and carried off to her long captivity. A hundred years or so later, Cromwell appeared on the scene and was defeated by the Scottish General Leslie on marshy ground west of Gogar and chased away to Dunbar. He left his mark, however, in the damage done to the church and its effigies by his men who were billeted there for a time.

The direct Forrester line continued until 1633 when George, the tenth baronet, was created Lord Forrester of Corstorphine by Charles I. This Lord George resigned the barony in favour of his brother, James Baillie, and his heirs, who also took the name of Forrester. This was confirmed by Charles II in 1651, the year of Lord George's death. His son, James, second Lord Forrester, was murdered by his niece beneath the Sycamore Tree on 20 August 1679 as will be told later. The Forrester line continued down the centuries and by various marriages came to the Earls of Verulam.

The story is now told in historic terms, illustrated as far as possible by relevant photographs and postcards. In publishing these photographs and notes, the Corstorphine Trust hopes that they will form something of a record of times and events that will show how the spirit of this community grew and still exists at the end of the twentieth century.

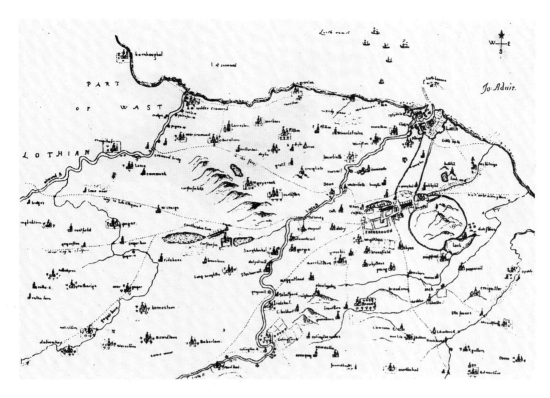

MAP OF MIDLOTHIAN BY JOHN ADAIR 1682
This shows the site of the Forrester Castle between Gogar and Corstorphine Lochs, but the relative sizes are not accurate. Corstorphine Loch was much the bigger and extended from the village as far east as modern Haymarket.

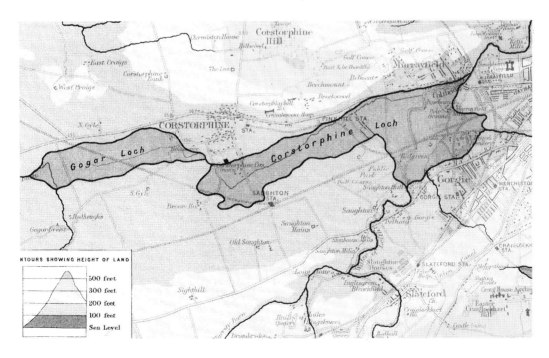

SITE OF ADAM FORRESTER'S CASTLE
This is indicated on this map from Cadell's *Story of the Forth* which also shows the relative sizes of the lochs.

CORSTORPHINE CASTLE *25 September 1837*
It stood about halfway along the present Castle Avenue and not a vestige of it remains. It provided a useful quarry for building stone in early Victorian times and many of the village houses and boundary walls were no doubt constructed from it.

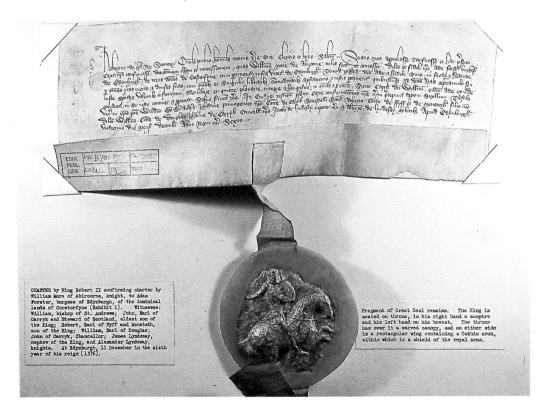

CHARTER by King Robert II confirming charter by William More of Abircorns, knight, to Adam Forrester, burgess of Edynburgh, of the dominical lands of Corstorfyne (Exhibit 1). Witnesses: William, bishop of St. Andrews; John, Earl of Carryk and Steward of Scotland, eldest son of the King; Robert, Earl of Fyff and Menateth, son of the King; William, Earl of Douglas; John of Carryk, Chancellor; James Lyndesay, nephew of the King, and Alexander Lyndesay, knights. At Edynburgh, 11 December in the sixth year of his reign [1376].

Fragment of Great Seal remains. The King is seated on throne, in his right hand a sceptre and his left hand on his breast. The throne has over it a carved canopy, and on either side is a rectangular wing containing a Gothic arch, within which is a shield of the royal arms.

THE CHARTER OF *1376*
King Robert II's Charter confirmed Adam Forrester's purchase of the Barony of Corstorphine from William More of Abercorn. (Now retained in the City Archives.)

HOW THE CASTLE MIGHT HAVE LOOKED IN ITS HEYDAY
(By kind permission of Yvonne de Cassablanca)

The castle was reckoned to be about 100 feet square with forty-foot-high circular towers at each corner with a moat fed from the loch adjacent to it. The living quarters were on the south side and it was approached by a two-arched bridge across the moat. It was used until the middle of the eighteenth century and then became a ruin.

THE TOMB OF SIR ADAM FORRESTER
This tomb in the south transept of the church, was defaced by Cromwell's troops when they were billeted there in 1650. The Scottish General Leslie had a battle with Cromwell's men on marshy ground near the site of the small golf course to the west of Gogar.

DOVECOT
The dovecot in Dovecot Road remains as a direct link with the Forresters and their castle. It is in an excellent state of repair and has over 1,000 nesting boxes for the birds which, in historic times, provided a welcome change of diet from salt beef in winter.

THE SYCAMORE TREE

This tree (*Acer Pseudoplatanus Corstorphinense*) is reckoned to be at least 600 years old and is a distinct variety of *acer* which bears brilliant yellow leaves in spring. At the turn of the century several scions were taken and these are to be found in local sites, notably one at the west entrance to St Anne's and another at the Kirk Stile in the High Street.

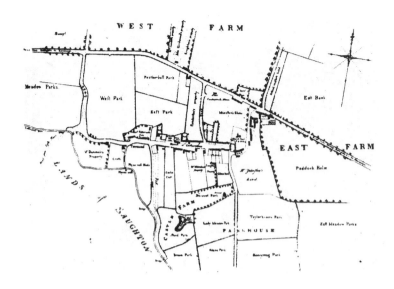

MAP OF THE VILLAGE 1771
This is the earliest accurate map of the village and shows the recently constructed highway, now St John's Road, with trees along its north boundary.

THE STANK BURN
This burn was cut in the latter half of the seventeenth century and drained the lochs, resulting in first-class farming land being formed. Redheughs, South Gyle, Broomhouse, Lairdship and Meadowhouse farms were the result . . . now all covered with bricks and concrete!

CORSTORPHINE FRIENDLY SOCIETY 1789

The increased prosperity of the village after the lochs were drained and agriculture began to flourish caused some of the more thinking men to realise that if they fell ill or were unable to work, hardship would follow. So, on 4 August 1789, they met and drew up Articles, a draft copy of which still exists. One of the first things they instigated was the purchase of this box with three locks. The Articles state that there is to be a Boxmaster and three Keymasters, with one key each.

THE ARTICLES

The Articles were agreed and state that the Society would be open to: '(1) men of decent character between ages 18 and 50 years; (2) none to be admitted who is of weak or sickly constitution or who has any "known trouble or distemper"; (3) must give full proof of his honesty and sobriety and shall contribute 2/6 entrance money and pay 1/- quarterly.'

THE SOCIETY'S COLOURS
One of the conditions of membership was an obligation to attend the annual dinner of the Society in June each year or be fined 2s. 6d. At the annual meeting, the Society would set off round the local houses preceded by a band and, from 1808, by their colours which were 'rouped' to the highest bidder. These colours are now on view in the Ladywell Medical Centre.

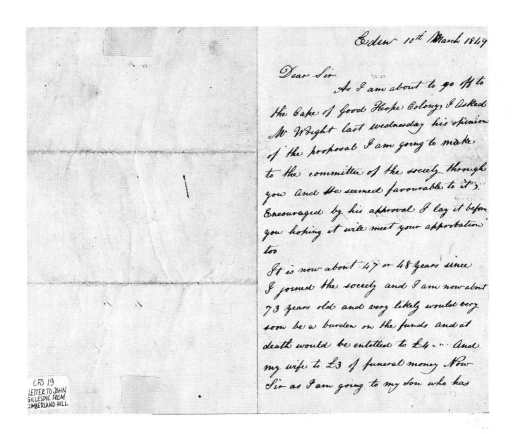

Eden 10th March 1849

Dear Sir

As I am about to go off to the Cape of Good Hope Colony, I asked Mr Wright last wednesday his opinion of the proposal I am going to make to the committee of the society through you And He seemed favourable to it). Encouraged by his approval I lay it before you hoping it will meet your approbation too

It is now about 47 or 48 years since I joined the society and I am now about 73 years old and very likely would very soon be a burden on the funds and at death would be entitled to £4... And my wife to £3 of funeral money Now Sir as I am going to my Son who has

kindly offered to keep his Father & Mother for the remainder of their days And as our finances are rather low to provide little comforts on the voyage which old people require if you would be so kind as grant me £5... out of the £7 I shall trouble you no more Please let me know your decision as soon as possible as I expect to sail about the end of next week Mr Wright will perhaps be so kind as bring me the news on wednesday — Now if you will grant me this favour you will confer a lasting obligation on your

Humble Servant

Cumberland Hill

at Mr A Nimmo's 45 Hope Park End

To John Gillespie Esqr Presit of the Friendly Benefit Society Corstorphine

P S You would require to appoint another to the office of visiting Steward for Edinburgh

C H —

A PLEA FROM A MEMBER 10 March 1849

21

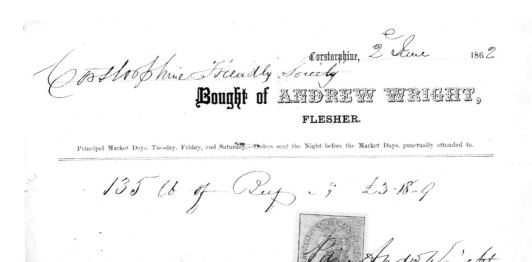

ONE OF THE BILLS FOR SUPPLIES FOR THEIR ANNUAL DINNER 1862
135 lb beef — £3 18s. 9d.

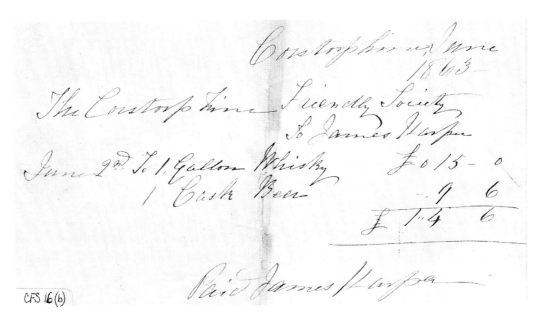

ANOTHER ACCOUNT
This time for one gallon of whisky at 15s., and a cask of beer at 9s. 6d.

Corstorphine 28th May 1844

Musicians *We hereby agree to furnish Twelve efficient clean & well dressed in uniform to play at The Corstorphine Friendly Society's General Meeting on Tuesday the 4th instant for the sum of Three pounds Sterling to be in attendance by 10 OClock AM any of the party getting himself the worse of drink to forfeit to the Society his pay*

James Mason

THE CONTRACT FOR THE HIRE OF THE BAND 1844
There is a note in the 1843 minutes about some unruly behaviour. This time they were taking no chances.

THE PARADE OF THE FRIENDLY SOCIETY c. 1898
They started in front of Corstorphine House with the pipe band from the Industrial School which occupied what is now Barnardo's offices in St John's Road.

THE BELL

Gifted to the church in 1577 by Sir James Forrester, the original bell was in use for 150 years. However, in 1728 the Kirk Session reported that it was 'rent' and 'of no use', and a new bell, this one, weighing 384 lbs. including the metal from the old one, was cast. It is still in use today and except for during the two World Wars it has been rung each Sunday since 1728.

THE PARISH CHURCH CHOIR c. 1870

The conductor was Mr Mollison, father of Bobbie Mollison who until 1978 had Woodbine Nursery.

THE PARISH CHURCH IN VICTORIAN TIMES

In 1828 William Burn, the architect, carried out extensive alterations, turning the chancel into a vestibule and breaking out a main entrance below the east window as shown here. A gallery was inserted across the nave with access to it via a wooden stair where the chancel arch now is. The pulpit was placed to the north of the tower.

BLACK BULL INN

This inn, at the corner of North Saughton Road and the High Street, was where James, Lord Forrester, was alleged to have been drinking on the night when he and his niece, Christian Nimmo, had their fatal quarrel and she murdered him with his sword beneath the Sycamore tree. She was beheaded at the Cross of Edinburgh three months later, on 12 November 1679.

THE SCHOOL-ROOM CHURCH
The event known as the Disruption of the Church of Scotland took place on 18 May 1843 and on 28 May a small band of thirty-six people of Corstorphine Church met in a small school-room adjacent to Mr Lind's bakery shop (now the Save the Children shop) opposite Manse Road, and so formed the first Free Church of Scotland in Corstorphine. Services were maintained weekly by ministers sent out from Edinburgh.

THE FIRST FREE CHURCH OF SCOTLAND
The school-room rapidly became too small and, for a time, services had to be held in a tent, first in a vacant site opposite the Parish School and later in a field on Bank Farm at the west end of the village. Early in 1844 the Revd Dr Burns (who had 'come out' from the Parish of Tweedsmuir) was inducted to be the first minister of the Free Church of Corstorphine. The first stone church was begun on a site next to the school-room and opened in May 1844.

THE FREE CHURCH GROWS

By 1869 the congregation had outgrown the small building and it was decided to enlarge the building by widening it sideways, extending it northwards, heightening the roof, and introducing a gallery. In 1886, when it received the gift of an American organ, an apse was built to the north and the church was given its rectangular shape.

THE CARNEGIE ORGAN

At the union with the U.P. Church in 1900 the Church became the United Free Church, and, about the same time, it received the gift of a pipe organ from Mr Andrew Carnegie. This was placed directly in front of the pulpit until, in 1912, a further enlargement took place when transepts were added to increase the seating and the organ was moved to its present position in the east transept.

AND TODAY

By 1943 when the Church's centenary came round, the Second World War was on and it was decided to postpone celebrations. In 1953 the Kirk Session had asked me to carry out the redesigning of the nave to provide a centre aisle, design new furniture and seating, and to redecorate the Church.

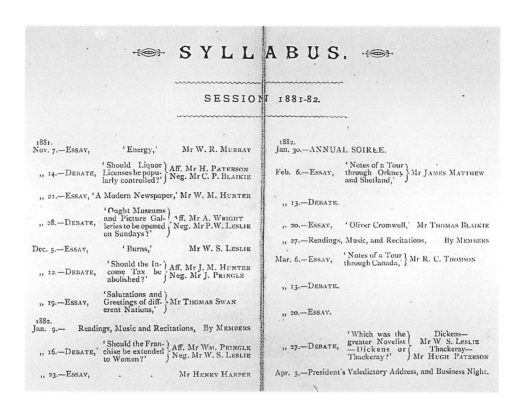

SYLLABUS.

SESSION 1881-82.

1881.
Nov. 7.—ESSAY, 'Energy,' Mr W. R. MURRAY

,, 14.—DEBATE, 'Should Liquor Licenses be popularly controlled?' Aff. Mr H. PATERSON / Neg. Mr C. P. BLAIKIE

,, 21.—ESSAY, 'A Modern Newspaper,' Mr W. M. HUNTER

,, 28.—DEBATE, 'Ought Museums and Picture Galleries to be opened on Sundays?' Aff. Mr A. WRIGHT / Neg. Mr P. W. LESLIE

Dec. 5.—ESSAY, 'Burns,' Mr W. S. LESLIE

,, 12.—DEBATE, 'Should the Income Tax be abolished?' Aff. Mr J. M. HUNTER / Neg. Mr J. PRINGLE

,, 19.—ESSAY, 'Salutations and Greetings of different Nations,' Mr THOMAS SWAN

1882.
Jan. 9.— Readings, Music and Recitations, By MEMBERS

,, 16.—DEBATE, 'Should the Franchise be extended to Women?' Aff. Mr WM. PRINGLE / Neg. Mr W. S. LESLIE

,, 23.—ESSAY, . . Mr HENRY HARPER

1882.
Jan. 30.—ANNUAL SOIRÉE.

Feb. 6.—ESSAY, 'Notes of a Tour through Orkney and Shetland,' Mr JAMES MATTHEW

,, 13.—DEBATE.

,, 20.—ESSAY, 'Oliver Cromwell,' Mr THOMAS BLAIKIE

,, 27.—Readings, Music, and Recitations, By MEMBERS

Mar. 6.—ESSAY, 'Notes of a Tour through Canada,' Mr R. C. THOMSON

,, 13.—DEBATE.

,, 20.—ESSAY.

,, 27.—DEBATE, 'Which was the greater Novelist —Dickens or Thackeray?' Dickens— Mr W. S. LESLIE / Thackeray— Mr HUGH PATERSON

Apr. 3.—President's Valedictory Address, and Business Night.

'THE LIT'

In 1880, in the back room of a tailor's shop (Wallace) in the High Street, a Literary Association was formed. It was a very successful venture and soon gathered a wide circle of members. Around the end of the century the Dey family came to the village, Mr James Dey (senior), my father's cousin, opening a stationer's business opposite Manse Road. His son James, better known as Jimmy Dey, was President on several occasions during the next thirty years, and his brother, John, was Treasurer during that period. Both took part in the social life of the village. The Corstorphine Literary and Geographical Association still meets every Monday evening throughout the winter, when audiences in the region of 200 people hear a number of speakers on a variety of subjects. As will be seen from this 1881-82 syllabus, debates were favourite events.

NINETEENTH-CENTURY BOWLING
The Bowling Club began about 1890 when Mr Pringle Taylor allowed games to be played on his private green at Dunsmuir.

QUOITS

The Quoiting Club was also formed in the 1890s and had two pitches, one at Ladywell and one near the Smiddy. Several 'kites' have been preserved by the Trust — solid iron rings about ten inches in diameter made by the blacksmith. Some are lying in front of the group.

. . . AND TENNIS

Tennis, too, was popular in the 1890s and the Tennis Club at that time rented a grass court in the north-west corner of what is now Union Park, then the Edinburgh University Playing Field. The club was a very enthusiastic company and made great efforts at the time to raise money to purchase their own ash courts.

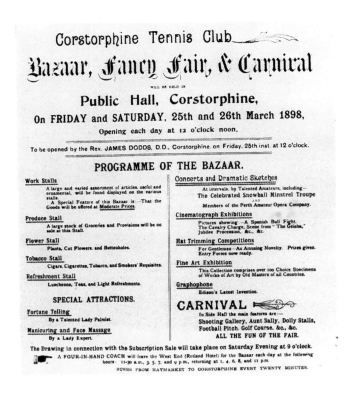

BAZAAR, FANCY FAIR AND CARNIVAL 1898

The Tennis Club's big Bazaar, Fancy Fair and Carnival was advertised all over Edinburgh and a four-in-hand coach ran from the West End and regular horse buses left from Haymarket. This effort was completely successful and raised enough money to enable the club to acquire ground in Belgrave Road and construct ash courts and a pavilion. The courts are now all-weather and the club still flourishes.

MORE FUND-RAISING

This is an advertisement for one of the club's biggest efforts to raise money. Note the instructions in the left and right bottom corners.

A DAY TRIP, 1890s STYLE
A very popular event each year at this time was the annual outing of the Burns Club. This outing of twenty-five men, thirty-four ladies and four children, was to Inversnaid. The parish minister, Revd James Fergusson, is in the second back row.

A BURNS CLUB OUTING TO POOSIE NANSIE'S INN
Thirty-six men, twenty-three ladies, five pipers and one child in arms: there is no sign of the minister this time!

THE HORSE BUS SERVICE
This began in 1881. It operated from the bus station and stables in St John's Road opposite Victor Park Terrace. There was one bus per hour and the fare to Haymarket was 1s. inside and 6d. on top. It was a rival to the train which ran from the station at Saughton on the Glasgow line, a mile from the village.

HARP HOTEL AND BUS c. 1900

ANY MORE FARES?
The Coltbridge-Corstorphine bus outside the Oak Inn c. 1895. There seem to be a lot of 6d. passengers and few inside at 1s. Perhaps it is just the presence of the photographer! City cable trams had been extended to Coltbridge at Wester Coates and met this bus.

OFF TO SCHOOL
The earliest school is thought to have been a one-roomed building which probably stood where Albyn Cottage now stands in the High Street. In 1819 the schoolmaster's glebe or lampacre was established here and this public school was built. It was extended in 1848 and in 1897.

THE PUBLIC SCHOOL 1872
Before the Education Act of 1874, the responsibility for education passed from the Kirk Session and came under the State.

THE MANSIONHOUSE

This was built in 1746 out of the ruins of the castle, by a Leith timber merchant, as a lodging house for visitors to the Well of Corstorphine, which was situated behind Dunsmuir and which had a wide reputation for its healing properties. People came from all over Scotland to drink the waters and horse buses were run from Edinburgh several times daily at this time.

THE PHYSIC WELL

In the late seventeenth and early eighteenth centuries one of the many wells in the district was known as the Physic Well, located at the south-east of Dunsmuir Estate. It gained a great reputation for its curative properties and people came from all parts to take the waters.

ST JOHN'S ROAD IN THE 1890s

Clermiston Road is on the right with Liddle's Dairy on the corner. Beyond are Steven's bakery and Three-Mile House. The horse bus is coming along past a woman in a shawl sitting on the shaft of her cart, whilst beyond is a barrel water-cart.

ADAM DUNN'S BAKERY AT No. 64 ST JOHN'S ROAD
Still a bakery using the same bakehouse, it is now Donachie's. Note the ventilated bread vans about
to set off on their delivery rounds.

ST JOHN'S ROAD AGAIN

Here is another view of Three-Mile House where Mr Douglas Brown, the donor of St Margaret's Park, stayed. The row of cottages and small shops were removed in 1922 to allow the tramcars to pass. Behind was the village slaughterhouse.

THE GLEBE 1894

The path in the centre led from the manse to a gate in the north wall of the churchyard and was known as 'the Minister's roadie'. Note the lack of a door in what is now the entrance to the church. At this time it was the vestry.

LABURNUM COTTAGE, ST JOHN'S ROAD
Miss Scott's grocery shop was at the extreme right of the picture.

THE GLEBE FROM MISS SCOTT'S SHOP

CORMACK, THE CHEMIST, BEFORE THE FRONT WAS ADDED, c. 1898
Note the legend on the fanlight above the door which reads 'Teeth carefully extracted'.

CORMACK, THE CHEMIST
The interior of the shop as it remained well into this century.

HARP HOTEL c. *1896*
Before any alterations.

BELLWOOD

Charles Smith, the joiner, is attending to repairs to a gig. The pantiled building is his workshop although it is now a vet's surgery. St Ninian's Drive now joins St John's Road just beyond, where the tree is, and beyond that is the Smiddy and its copper-beech tree.

THE SMIDDY

Underneath the spreading beechnut tree, which still survives, Hugh Kerr, the blacksmith, sits on the left, with Dr Matthew's groom and horse in the centre. The Smiddy was active until 1922 before becoming a lawnmower depot and eventually Ransome's main Scottish HQ. The site was cleared in the 1960s and a petrol station established.

FERRYBANK
For many years a market garden, and demolished along with the Smiddy next door, it is now part of the modern petrol station. Behind the house was the Bee Wall.

THE BEE WALL
This suffered the same fate as Ferrybank and the Smiddy and became part of the petrol station. It had been constructed in the late eighteenth century when Ferrybank was occupied by a candlemaker and this was his source of beeswax. There was room for about a dozen 'skeps', lodged on the north side with the bees flying in and out via small slits on the south side.

T. W. BEACH & SON'S ESTABLISHMENT AT THE TURN OF THE CENTURY
The old house was superseded by the present building in 1906 and the business was only closed in
1989. Mr Beach is standing at the right of the doorway in his shirt-sleeves. Note the rolls of lead on
the lorry.

THE FREE CHURCH AGAIN
The Sunday School picnic of 1900 on its way along the High Street bound for Gogar Burn at
Redheughs Farm. Note the piper in the second cart.

ANOTHER PICNIC
This Free Church outing is possibly heading for Dalmeny which was a favourite picnic place for
many years.

FRONT VIEW OF CORSTORPHINE HILL HOUSE c. 1900
It was extensively remodelled about three years later.

BACK VIEW OF THE HOUSE BEFORE ALTERATIONS
The zoo took over in 1910 and it became the Fellows' Club House, opened in 1913.

MISS SCOTT'S SUNDAY SCHOOL CLASS AT A PICNIC
Note the wee lad on the right, complete with kilt, plaid and sporran!

MR WALKER OF AVONBANK DRIVING OFF FROM THE FIRST TEE 1903
From 1902 until 1928 there was a very popular nine-hole golf course on Corstorphine Hill on what
is now the upper part of the zoo. It had an active membership and its clubhouse and first tee were
at the east end of Old Kirk Road. The lease expired in 1928 and it moved out to Ratho Park where
it had more room. Onlookers include the schoolmaster Mr McGown, Dr Malcolmson, Jimmy Dey
and John Wallace (senior).

CORSTORPHINE POST OFFICE, BELGRAVE PLACE 1903
Standing proudly in front, from left to right, are: Robert McDuff (the telegram boy), William Pattullo, William Brown, Miss Forrest, Miss C. Millar, Miss N. McLeish, Miss C. Millar, Miss A. Rodger, (unknown), and Mr Waddell (the postmaster).

ELECTION 1906 — USHER'S ROOM ON RIGHT

TOP OF KIRK LOAN 1903
John Brown's delivery cart is just passing Dickson's Dairy across the road.

LADYWELL COTTAGES c. *1902*

A favourite scene for artists during the last century. The cottages and trees were cleared away in 1953 to widen the road and enable the south end of Featherhall Avenue to join the High Street. The proposal raised a great protest and the authorities had to produce a much better scheme than what was originally envisaged.

KEEPING LEFT DIDN'T SEEM TO MATTER IN 1905
Mr and Mrs W. Brown of Sycamore Terrace out for a run in the wide open spaces of West Craigs
Road. Mr Brown was an amateur photographer in the early part of this century and took many
photos which became picture postcards, many of which are in this collection. The small child on
the handlebars is his son, Gow, who became a noted Heriot's rugby player in the 1920s.

MR BROWN AGAIN, WITH GOW ON THE HANDLEBARS, IN BROOMHOUSE ROAD
Castle Park is in the middle distance and, behind, the slopes of Corstorphine Hill are devoid of
houses. The road with the trees, is the Farm Road, now Old Kirk Road.

PUBLIC SCHOOL c. 1905
The school was extended to two storeys in 1897. The schoolmaster's house is behind the tree on the left.

PUBLIC SCHOOL CLASS c. 1911 WITH MR McGOWN, HEADMASTER, ON THE RIGHT

THE WIDOWERS' CHILDREN'S HOME AND THE 'CONVALESCENT' HOME
The Widowers' Children's Home, now Barnardo's HQ, is on the left, with the 'Convalescent' Home in the centre and Corstorphine Hill House, now the Zoo Club House, in the distance. This is before the railway was built across the foreground.

THE RESTORED PARISH CHURCH
In 1905 the Parish Church was restored when the door in the east gable was built up. The slated roofs of 1828 were replaced with concrete slabs to simulate the 1429 stone slabs on the chancel and the south transept roofs.

AN EARLY LORRY
One of the first motor lorries in the district, owned by Mr Dick, a slater, and then by Mr Beach,
plumber.

SAUGHTON ROAD WITH DOVECOT ROAD ON THE RIGHT c. *1909*

THE VIEW SOUTH

Looking across from Mr W. Brown's house to Craiglockhart Hydropathic, Saughton Station (formerly Corstorphine Station) is in the middle-distance with the Royal High School pavilion, now Union Park, in front. The rest of the foreground is now Tyler's Acre housing. The Stank Burn is where the three bushes are.

APPROACHING THE STATION FROM PINKHILL
Corstorphine had very long platforms, especially in the goods yard, as during the 1890s there was talk of new cavalry barracks being sited at the west of the village to replace Piershill Barracks. In fact, they went to Redford instead. The long platforms allowed the mainline trains to be washed and cleaned here in later years.

THE 1.10 FROM WAVERLEY c. 1909
The journey took only fourteen minutes and allowed passengers to come home for lunch and still be back within the hour!

ST ANNE'S CHURCH

In 1895 it was decided that much needed extra seating accommodation could not be provided in the Parish Church and that a new church would have to be built. In 1902 a site at Belgrave Park was obtained and a wood and iron temporary church was built and opened in 1903 with 398 seats.

ST ANNE'S SUNDAY SCHOOL 1908

The Revd John A. Robertson was called to be minister at St Anne's Church and began his ministry there in May 1903. He was an exceptional man and built up a congregation rapidly. This is the Sunday School in 1908 with some of their teachers. Mr Robertson is seated with the Revd Mr Anderson who was a member and became the 'Father' of the Church of Scotland. The girl on Mr Robertson's left is his daughter, Aileen, who became Lady Slim, wife of Viscount Slim of Burma.

THE STONE CHURCH

From 1906 this stone church was the target set for the small congregation. By 1911 Mr Macgregor Chalmers had been appointed architect and, with the close co-operation of Mr Robertson, he produced this magnificent design for one of the finest church buildings in Scotland. Unfortunately, owing to the outbreak of the Great War, the campanile was not built.

THE FOUNDATION STONE OF ST ANNE'S CHURCH

This was laid on 25 May 1912 with a great gathering of Corstorphine people. In the company can be seen Mr McGown, the Revd James Ferguson, the Revd Peter Beith, Mr Robertson, and the Moderator, the Rt Revd Marcus Dill DD, who conducted the service. The stone was laid by the Rt Hon. Lord Dunedin, Lord President of the Court of Session.

THE TYMPANUM OF ST ANNE'S DOORWAY

This shows Christ in Glory seated on the Rainbow, with the world in one hand and the other raised in blessing and surrounded by the four evangelists. Round the main panel are the seven angels with their candles. Below, round the door, are the signs of the zodiac with the Lamb and the Cross in the middle. This is one of the most elaborately carved doors in the country. Inside there is more carved stone of the same character and eighteen stained-glass windows of superb quality. St Anne's is an architectural gem that all Corstorphine residents can be proud of.

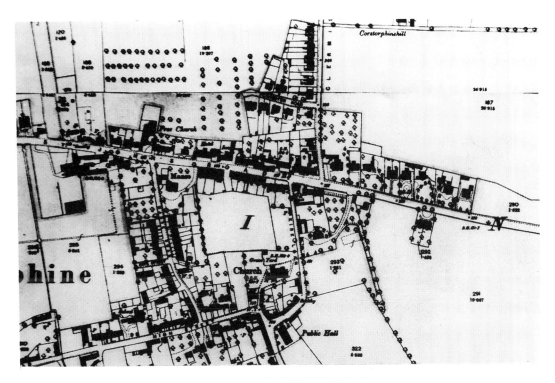

ORDNANCE SURVEY MAP OF 1895

Before the direct railway line, the station was still at Saughton on the Glasgow line. The houses had spread eastwards as far as No. 22 St John's Road. Belgrave House stands where Belgrave Terrace now is, and the glebe between Manse Road and Kirk Loan is still not built on. Corstorphine Hill Farm, on the north side of Old Kirk Road, was known as the Farm Road.

CORSTORPHINE RANGERS FOOTBALL TEAM c. 1911
Back row: Robertson, Steedman, Glendinning, Arthur, Burnet, Bowick, Kilgour
Middle row: Steedman, Riddle, Paterson, Rae, Forrest, Calder, Gilroy, McLeish, Donaldson
Front row: Campbell, Wallace, Hossack, McIntosh, Wight, Scobie, Kidd, Dickson

THE EDINBURGH SCHOOL OF GARDENING

At the east end of Old Kirk Road the Edinburgh School of Gardening was established by Miss Morrison in the early years of this century. By 1914 it was training young ladies to be what became known as 'land girls' to take the place of men who had gone to the war. Kaimes Road was extended northwards in about 1930, through the site of the greenhouses, to meet Cairnmuir Road.

AT WORK ON THE FRUIT GARDEN

RAISING SEEDLINGS IN THE GLASSHOUSES

PUPILS DISPLAY AT THE OPENING OF THE SCHOOL EXTENSION 1910

SCHOOL EXTENSION 1910
The Parish Council party at its opening. *Left to right:* George Sutherland (scoutmaster),
Sir Robert Boothby, Revd J. A. Robertson (St Anne's), Mr Oliphant, Miss Kerr (schoolboard),
Mrs Tod, Revd P. Beith (U.F. Church), Hugh Paterson, Miss Inglis, Mr McGown (headmaster),
Tom Keir (janitor), Mr Galloway (scout).

THE GATES OPEN
The inauguration of St Margaret's Park in July 1915 by Mrs Douglas Brown. Her husband had bought
nursery ground to the south of the High Street and presented the park to the village.

MR DOUGLAS BROWN ADDRESSING THE PARTY

A PRESENTATION
Mrs Douglas Brown receiving a bouquet from a boy scout. The Revd and Mrs Fergusson are on the left, with the Revd Peter Beith at the back.

THE NEUK
Established at the end of the Great War their tearooms were greatly used by cyclists and hikers as
the start and finish of their outings.

SIDNEY SALMON'S STUDIO IN MANSE ROAD
Mr Salmon was a commercial photographer, photographing people in the days when few people used
cameras. He is responsible for many of the photos we have of the village *c.* 1895 - *c.* 1912.

THE MAN WITH THE BEAR
He came to the school occasionally to amuse the children and then take a walk around Clermiston and Gordon Roads etc.

CORSTORPHINE AMBULANCE UNIT
During the war years this was the ambulance unit based at Mr Tod's home, Clerwood, which was a military hospital from 1917-20. His daughter, Dr Tod, was very much liked by the men and, after the war, was interested in providing activities for ex-servicemen.

ANTI-AIRCRAFT UNIT
After the April 1916 Zeppelin raid on Edinburgh, an anti-aircraft unit was established on the rocky knoll to the west of Rest and Be Thankful, complete with searchlight crew. It was manned by regulars and local territorials.

BEECHWOOD CORNER ON CORSTORPHINE ROAD WITH TREES ALONG THE SOUTH SIDE

The road was increased in width and a retaining wall built from Balgreen to Pinkhill in 1922 to allow for widening and the tramcars to be brought out from Saughtonhall to the zoo and then to Corstorphine.

COMMENDATION FROM THE PEOPLE

This is a copy of an 'Illuminated Address' presented to Lieut David Macintyre VC in November 1918 by the people of Corstorphine in recognition of his achievement. It is signed by the ministers of the Corstorphine churches and by the chief officials of the Parish Council. Mr Macintyre spent his school days with his aunt in Downie Terrace and attended the United Free Church (St Ninians). After the war he entered the Civil Service first in London and later as head of the Ministry of Works in Edinburgh.

MOUND, HAYMARKET, MURRAYFIELD AND CORSTORPHINE
The first SMT bus service from the Royal Scottish Academy in 1908 with driver, William Thomson, who became Lord Provost 1932. Note the solid tyres and the chain drive to the back wheels. Third from the right inside is John Dey, Jimmy Dey's brother.

MR HERD AND HIS 'WEE BUS'
Between 1918 and 1923 when electric trams were extended, first to the zoo and then to Station Road, Corstorphine, Mr Herd ran this service from the 'old car terminus' to the zoo. During the train strike of October 1919, people had to walk each morning to the cable-car terminus at Saughtonhall.

THE FIRST TRAMCAR, 22 June 1923
Electric trams superseded the cable system in 1922. The lines were extended from Saughtonhall, the cable-car terminus, in 1922/23, first to the zoo, then, on 22 June, to Station Road and subsequently to the Neuk crossroads, Drumbrae, finally reaching the Maybury in 1936. They were discontinued in 1956.

THE FIRST CORPORATION BUS SERVICE TO CORSTORPHINE
Edinburgh absorbed Corstorphine in 1920 and provided a bus service to Drumbrae using second-hand London vehicles. This one is standing at the crossroads at the foot of Drumbrae Road; Craigs Road and Bank Farm are on the right in the distance.

CORSTORPHINE STATION AND WAR MEMORIAL
The large open area in front of the station was the site of the War Memorial erected in 1919. In 1928
it was re-sited opposite the new library in Kirk Loan.

CLERMISTON ROAD c. 1920
There is still no building on the east side beyond Old Kirk Road, the lampposts are in scale with their
surroundings, Brown the Grocer's delivery cart and Mr Waddell's telegraph boy are on their way.

SPORTING INTERESTS

In 1920 the Corstorphine Amateur Athletic Association was formed by local enthusiasts, amongst whom Dr Margaret Tod of Clerwood was prominent. The Corstorphine Swifts, a soccer club, had much success in playing junior teams from West Lothian and round about.

84

G. J. COOKE — TOBACCONIST, NEWSAGENT AND CONFECTIONER
Another instance of Dr Margaret Tod's regard for ex-servicemen after the First World War was when
she helped Mr Cooke open his successful shop opposite the foot of Clermiston Road. It was much
patronised in the 1930s when one could buy a fourpenny poke of sweets, a green *Sports Dispatch*, two
ninepenny tickets at the Astoria and still have change from two shillings!

CORSTORPHINE BOWLING CLUB c. 1923
In the centre, in front of the flagpole, is Mr W. H. Scouller, who was eleven-times champion of the green, six times in the finals of the Scottish Championship at Queen's Park and was captain of the Scottish team in 1920 and 1921.

CORSTORPHINE ATHLETIC FOOTBALL CLUB
The team that won the Bathgate Trophy in 1926.

VIEW FROM CLERMISTON ROAD c. *1920*
Saughton Road runs behind the trees, across the picture, to Saughton Station, on the far side of the
Union Park pavilion (at that time the Royal High School Playing Fields). The large wooded area
beyond was known as the Plantation; now it is occupied by Government offices and has only one
tree remaining! Beyond are the plantations on the slopes of Capelaw Hill in the Pentlands.

ST JOHN'S ROAD LOOKING WEST FROM THE TOP OF KIRK LOAN c. 1920
The cottages on the right were cleared away in 1922 to widen the road for tramcars, and the United
Free Church tower in the background is now St Ninian's. There is such a busy bus stop on the corner
today that no one would think of stooping to tie a shoelace at this spot!

HALL TERRACE IN SAUGHTON ROAD, DEMOLISHED c. 1950

NORTH END OF HALL TERRACE AT THE IRISH CORNER
The cottage on the left still stands, renovated as a house after serving for some years as the Royal British Legion Hall. Kirk Loan is on the right. All the Irish Corner property was demolished in 1932 and the view of the Parish Church from the south revealed.

PADDOCKHOLM CROFT
Positioned at the south end of Kirk Loan it was demolished to clear the site for the library in 1936.

The Oldest House in Corstorphine

THE OLDEST HOUSE IN CORSTORPHINE
Claycot Dairy was a flourishing establishment from Victorian times until quite recently. The house has now become the administration unit at the centre of the Claycot Retirement Complex.

'PHEMIE' THE FISHWIFE
The village fishwife, 'Phemie', with Mrs Walker, down a pend off the High Street, now Augustine House. Note the standpipe on the right.

MISS SCOTT'S CLASS IN THE U.F. CHURCH SUNDAY SCHOOL c. 1923
Miss Scott, who had a grocery shop in Laburnum Cottages, kept a lot of photographs and cuttings
about Corstorphine from about 1890 onwards and these have now been mounted into a large book
in the Trust's possession.

MISS GUN'S PRIVATE SCHOOL AT 18 ST JOHN'S ROAD c. 1919
Many residents may still recognise themselves.

MISS GUN'S SCHOOL AGAIN c. *1926*
Even more people will recognise themselves, with Miss Gun sitting on the right and Miss Elizabeth
on the left.

CLERMISTON ROAD c. *1914*
The valley is now practically all built over. The little figure in front is Gow Brown.

CRAIGS ROAD c. *1929*
In the distance the first houses on the west side of Drumbrae Road can be seen.

TENTH MIDLOTHIAN SCOUT TROOP c. *1922*

Corstorphine's boys took to scouting very early on in the Scout Movement's history and the Tenth Midlothian Troop were registered as No. 10 Troop of Baden Powell's Boy Scouts at the London headquarters in 1907. After the Great War Mr Douglas Brown, the donor of St Margaret's Park, had one of the Cross Cottages near the park renovated to become a scout hall and presented it to the troop. Here is part of the troop with their trekcart. On the right is patrol leader Gow Brown, very much grown-up now!

THE TENNIS CLUB 1922
Some are still to the fore — but not playing now!

THE TENNIS CLUB c. *1926*

THE TENNIS CLUB 1938
It was quite hard to get admitted in those days and it was a very busy place. A good marriage market too!

STANK BURN FLOOD, September 1927
This photograph shows how Stank Burn, neglected by the city authorities and silted up below the road bridges, caused flooding at Redheughs and Gogar. The area shown is now the site of the big roundabout at the north end of the city bypass.

PLUMBER'S HAYCART c. 1919
Mr Beach is giving a hand with the harvest. With him are his sons, George, standing, and Tom, sitting.

THE PARISH CHURCH BOYS' BRIGADE 1929
Capt. Frank Cowie, the Revd Oswald B. Milligan in the centre, and Morton Cowie.

CORSTORPHINE COTTAGES
This neat row of houses was demolished in about 1960 to allow Low's Supermarket to be built. The left-hand house belonged to Mr Downie and his descendants. For many years he was the village saddler and his shop was the building just visible on the left of the picture. It was entered from the top of Kirk Loan.

THE CRAIGMOUNT AREA
Bughtlin Burn runs beside the trees in the middle and in the distance is Drumbrae which looks almost flat. In the top right-hand corner are the two bungalows on the west side of Drumbrae, opposite the shops in Drumbrae Avenue.

A PANORAMIC VIEW OF SOUTH GYLE FARM 1963
The farm is in the trees to the right of Craigsbank Church tower; the farm cottages are to the right and the road to Gogar Burn — a favourite walk — lies between the Dalmeny and Glasgow lines below the gasometer. Sighthill estate is just beyond.

SOUTH GYLE FARMHOUSE
One of the most up-to-date houses in the district, it was abandoned to the vandals by the District
in 1967.

'THE GYLE HERD': NOTICE OF DRAFT SALE
After the Second World War, Mr W. H. Gray of South Gyle Farm established a noteworthy herd
of 'large white' pigs — 'the Gyle Herd' — which won champion awards all over Britain. The annual
draft sales in May in the early 1950s brought buyers from far and wide.

MR GRAY AT THE DRAFT SALE 1951
A section of the ring with Willie Gray on the extreme left next to the auctioneer.

CHAMPION PIG 1966

Mr Gray's daughter, Betty, became a pig-breeder in her own right and bred Wessex Saddleback pigs with great success in the 1960s. She won the Supreme Championship in the Wessex Class at the Royal Highland Show in 1966 with this Gyle, Landgirl 12th, and also the Oliver Cup in the same year. There were many noted pig-breeders in Corstorphine at this time, names like Baxter, Cowper of Gogar and Newbigging come to mind.

THE UNVEILING AND DEDICATION OF THE 1939-45 WAR MEMORIAL 8 May 1948
The Revd Professor James Barr is at the microphone with the Revd D. McArthur Chalmers of
Carrickknowe Church on his left. In front is the Lady Provost, Miss Rodney Murray, Field Marshal
Lord Slim, Lord Provost Andrew Murray and Lady Slim, daughter of Revd J. A. Robertson, first
minister of St Anne's.

THE 8.33 FROM CORSTORPHINE HEADING FOR BALGREEN HALT

THE 5.15 MAKING FOR PINKHILL

EVENING ARRIVALS, CORSTORPHINE STATION

THE OLD MANSE, SOUTH FRONT
This part was built about the 1830s, the bow windows being added in the 1880s. It was demolished in 1959 and a modern manse built on the site to the south. Some of the old stone was built into the new house.

THE OLD MANSE, NORTH FRONT
The oldest part dating from about 1650. It had no central heating but according to Dr Franklin, one of the most efficient systems of central cooling in the country!

DR FOSTER FRANKLIN AND HIS FAMILY AT THE OLD MANSE IN 1959

VIEW OF THE HILL FROM LADYWELL AVENUE c. 1953

BROOMHOUSE FARM, PRESENT SITE OF FORRESTER SCHOOL
The steading was behind, and Mr Boyd was the farmer in the 1920s and 1930s. Meadowplace Road
now comes in on the right and 'takes over' from Broomhouse Road.

HARVESTING AT EAST CRAIGS c. *1936*
Craigs Road is on the right.

HARVESTING AT EAST CRAIGS c. *1938*

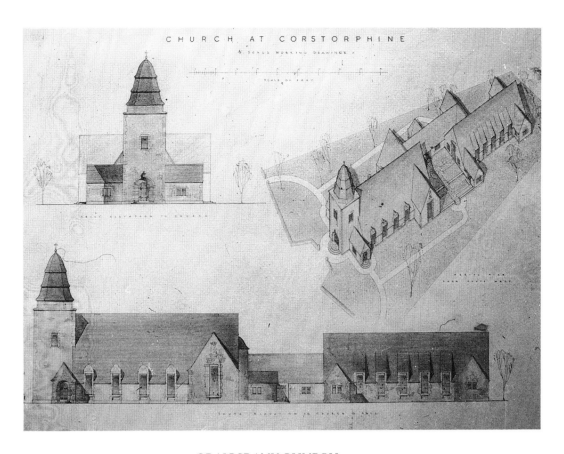

CRAIGSBANK CHURCH 1937
This was the original design in 1937, but it was enlarged in 1962 to a different design.

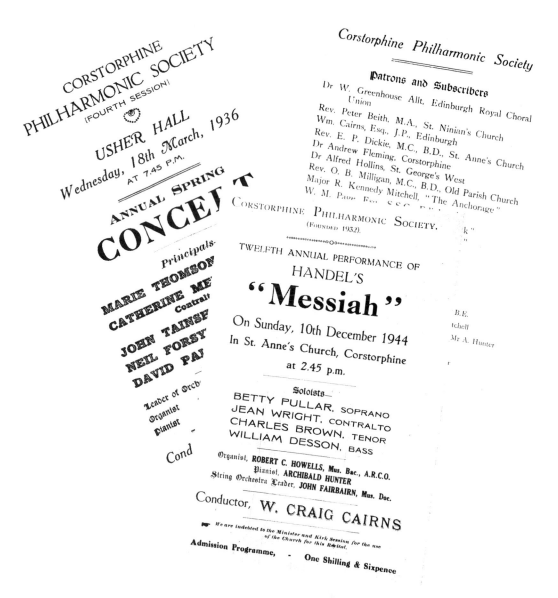

CORSTORPHINE PHILHARMONIC SOCIETY
(FOURTH SESSION)

USHER HALL
Wednesday, 18th March, 1936
AT 7.45 P.M.

ANNUAL SPRING CONCERT

Principals-
MARIE THOMSON
CATHERINE ME
Contral
JOHN TAINSF
NEIL FORSY
DAVID PA

Leader of Orch
Organist
Pianist

Cond

Corstorphine Philharmonic Society

Patrons and Subscribers
Dr W. Greenhouse Allt, Edinburgh Royal Choral
Union
Rev. Peter Beith, M.A., St. Ninian's Church
Wm. Cairns, Esq., J.P., Edinburgh
Rev. E. P. Dickie, M.C., B.D., St. Anne's Church
Dr Andrew Fleming, Corstorphine
Dr Alfred Hollins, St. George's West
Rev. O. B. Milligan, M.C., B.D., Old Parish Church
Major R. Kennedy Mitchell, "The Anchorage"
W. M. Page, Esq.

B.E.
tchell
Mr A. Hunter

CORSTORPHINE PHILHARMONIC SOCIETY.
(FOUNDED 1932).

TWELFTH ANNUAL PERFORMANCE OF
HANDEL'S
"Messiah"
On Sunday, 10th December 1944
In St. Anne's Church, Corstorphine
at 2.45 p.m.

Soloists-
BETTY PULLAR, SOPRANO
JEAN WRIGHT, CONTRALTO
CHARLES BROWN, TENOR
WILLIAM DESSON, BASS

Organist, ROBERT C. HOWELLS, Mus. Bac., A.R.C.O.
Pianist, ARCHIBALD HUNTER
String Orchestra Leader, JOHN FAIRBAIRN, Mus. Doc.

Conductor, W. CRAIG CAIRNS

We are indebted to the Minister and Kirk Session for the use
of the Church for this Recital.
Admission Programme, - One Shilling & Sixpence

THE ANNUAL EVENT 1944
Every December, the Society performed Handel's *Messiah* at St Anne's Church.

CREDITS FOR THE SPRING CONCERT 1936
This was a very ambitious affair with a concert version of *Merrie England*, many part songs and a choral waltz, 'Invitation to the Waltz'. For several years after the war the choir continued to lead the singing at the British Legion's Festival of Remembrance, in the Astoria Picture House each year.

THE CORSTORPHINE PHILHARMONIC SOCIETY
Formed in 1932 by the organist of the Parish Church, Mr W. Craig Cairns, and the organist of St Anne's, Mr Neil Heath Lees, it attracted singers from the three churches and others and proved a most successful body with a wide repertoire. The choir gave several recitals each year in the Usher Hall, Music Hall, and the Central Hall.

AN OUTING FROM THE ZOO
Corstorphine Zoo was opened in 1913 on the lower slopes of the Hill and was extended northward
in 1928 taking in the ground previously occupied by the golf course. From its earliest years it has been
famous for its collection of king penguins. They were the originators of the 'walkabout' and here they
are at the tram stop at the main gate.

ANOTHER CORSTORPHINE RESIDENT ON HIS BIKE
Philip, one of the chimpanzee family, was a great favourite with the public.

THE FOUNDER MEMBERS OF THE ROTARY CLUB, April 1955
Since that date the club has carried out many good works for the benefit of the community, notably the 'Know Your Neighbourhood' exhibition in 1958. There is also an Inner Wheel section and more recently a Probus Club for retired members. Included in the picture are W. Newbigging, A. Moyes, J. McNair, D. Banks, A. Murdoch, W. Crawford, J. Young, C. Robertson, M. Bowden, E. Cormack, J. Brown, A. Fairlie, Dr Franklin and Mr Hogarth.

THE OPENING OF THE FIRST 'KNOW YOUR NEIGHBOURHOOD' EXHIBITION
2-5 April, 1958
The fourteenth Lord Forrester helps to secure the success of this event with local industrial firms,
the armed forces, schools, churches and youth organisations all taking part.

THE PLATFORM PARTY
Left to right: Councillor Moncur, Councillor Matt Murray, the Lord Provost, Mr Martin Bowden
(President of the Rotary Club), Councillor David Kyles, and Dr Ernest Cormack with Lord Forrester
to the fore.

COMMEMORATING THE EXHIBITION, April 1958
Dr Cormack and Mr Martin Bowden at the tree planting in front of Corstorphine Church.

THE CHURCH FLOODLIT FOR THE EXHIBITION, April 1958

THE RUGBY CLUB 1951-52
The Corstorphine Amateur Athletic Association was formed in 1920 and gave rise to the Cricket, the Rugby and the Hockey Clubs. All were very active for many years and after a quiet spell the Rugby Club was reformed in 1950 with fixtures every Saturday. It has an interesting collection of photographs of past teams. This is one of the 'oldies'.

CORSTORPHINE LADIES' HOCKEY TEAM c. 1930
The Hockey Club too was an enthusiastic body formed from the Association, playing at Union Park.
Back row: Lily Burton, Cathy Wight, Edith Kidd, Nancy Johnstone, Sheila Stewart.
Front row: Freda Burton, N. Robertson, Mary Pollock, Winnie Kidd, Margaret Baxter.

TRAMCARS 'STACKED' AT THE NEUK, MURRAYFIELD RUGBY
INTERNATIONAL DAY 1936
When the signal came that the final whistle was about to be blown, the flood was released!

THE SCOTT TOWER AT CLERMISTON
Erected in 1871 by William McFie of Clermiston House to mark the centenary of Scott's birth, it was presented to the city in 1932 by Mr W. G. Walker to mark the centenary of Scott's death. It is one of the finest viewpoints in the country but is not now open to the public. The figure in front is Mr William Brown who is responsible for a number of the photographs in this collection.

THE PUBLIC HALL AND OLD LIBRARY
This was built in 1892, largely by the efforts of the Literary Association and still used for their weekly
meetings and for many other functions.

THE POSTCARDS

THE 'LOW' VILLAGE c. 1908
Note the bare feet. The 'Irish corner' houses are in the background.

THE ASTORIA PICTURE HOUSE IN MANSE ROAD
It opened in 1929, but closed on 29 June 1974.

THE HIGH STREET c. *1914*
Again, note the bare feet.

THE NEW ZOO ENTRANCE 1926
A loop line was made so that tramcars could wait clear of the service traffic.

THE 'CONVALESCENT' HOUSE BEFORE THE VERANDAHS WERE REMOVED

ST JOHN'S ROAD c. 1903
This part of St John's Road is where the pedestrian crossing now is. The date is about 1903 as the tenements at Belgrave Place are in the process of being built.

ST JOHN'S ROAD c. *1918*
The 'high' village as it was often referred to. No traffic!

ST JOHN'S ROAD c. *1930*
A quiet, peaceful street.

KAIMES ROAD c. *1910*
Note the greenhouses of the Edinburgh School of Gardening, known locally as 'the Lady Gardeners'. The road now continues through the site to Cairnmuir Road.

CLERMISTON AVENUE, NOW A WALKWAY

Gibson House or Dower House, Corstorphine
Albany Series

THE DOWER HOUSE
It is now thought more likely to have been a manse connected with the Collegiate Church. The house has now been fully restored and has become the headquarters of the Corstorphine Trust.

THE CORSTORPHINE TRUST

THE CORSTORPHINE TRUST has its origins in the wish of those who were brought together during the Second World War, serving on various capacities in Home Guard, ARP, Fire Watching, Observer Corps, Red Cross, and Civil Defence Organisations. A spirit of comradeship and mutual helpfulness had been engendered and many felt that this should be continued into peace time. So, at a public meeting on 1 June 1945, under the chairmanship of the Revd Prof. Allan Barr and addressed by Councillor Matt Murray, it was decided to form a Corstorphine District Association, with an annual subscription of one shilling!

The association was launched with a comprehensive constitution, nine kindred associations, a governing council of fifteen members plus office-bearers. This association was converted in 1970, largely by the enthusiasm of Dr Ernest Cormack, to be renamed The Corstorphine Trust and to have virtually the same objectives as in 1945, namely:

(a)   to stimulate public interest in, and care for, the beauty, history and character of Corstorphine and District;

(b)   to encourage the preservation, development and improvement of features of general public amenity or historic interest;

(c)   to promote or support activities having for their aims: (1) the welfare of the residents; (2) their cultural or educational advancement; (3) help for the sick, aged or infirm;

(d)   to promote the collection, preservation and display of objects of historical and local interest which may be acquired by, or gifted or loaned to the Trust;

(e)   to encourage high standards of architecture and town planning in Corstorphine and District;

(f)   to pursue these ends by means of meetings, exhibitions, lectures, publications, conferences and publicity, and the promotion of schemes of a charitable nature.

Now, in 1990, the kindred associations number thirty-three, including representatives of local churches, scouts, guides, the Women's Rural Institute, the Townswomen's Guild, and sports clubs, etc.

Over the years the Trust has dealt with many varied subjects, planning inquiries, traffic matters and, in the 1970s, carried out a feasibility study of the traffic problem on St John's Road which led, in the 1980s, to a firm project which was developed by the city authorities to relieve the congestion in Corstorphine and Gorgie by providing a road to the west to allow traffic to escape from the city without passing through these districts. The route had a long parliamentary inquiry and passage through both Houses of Parliament. Contracts were let and work about to begin when a change of administration in Lothian Regional Council in 1986 caused the whole scheme to be abandoned.

The pressure continues and the Trust has to keep a constant watchful eye out for developers ever anxious to build large office blocks which would ruin the amenity of the district and neighbourhood.

The Corstorphine Trust would like to pay tribute to Dr Ernest Cormack who has done so much in recent years in investigating the history of our village, collecting material relating to its past and allowing the Trust to occupy his premises at 199 St John's Road.

BIBLIOGRAPHY
Dey, W. G. — *St Anne's Parish Church*,
printed by Howie and Seath, Edinburgh, 1966.

Milligan, Rev. Oswald — *Corstorphine Parish Church*,
a Private Publication, Edinburgh, 1926.

Selway, G. Upton — *A Midlothian Village*,
Waterston, Edinburgh, 1890.

Thomson, D. — *The Corstorphine Heirloom*,
Featherhall Press, Corstorphine, 1948.